FICTION 🪶 A PRESENT FOR GRANNY

Written by Katherine Rawson
Illustrated by Ann Caranci

Chapter 1	At Granny's House	2
Chapter 2	Missing!	6
Chapter 3	Who Is the Thief?	10
Chapter 4	The Nest Sock	12

PIONEER VALLEY EDUCATIONAL PRESS, INC.

CHAPTER 1 🪶 AT GRANNY'S HOUSE

Granny's needles clicked rapidly through loops of bright red yarn. Meg sat on the sofa beside her, stroking Mimi, Granny's big orange cat. She felt so cozy on the sofa with Mimi on her lap and Granny close by. She snuggled against the cushions like a little bird tucked into its nest.

Meg's little brother, Alex, was sprawled on the carpet, leafing through a thick book.

"What are you reading?" asked Meg.

Alex showed her the cover: *The Big Book of Knots*.

"I didn't know you were interested in knots," said Meg.

"I didn't know I was either," said Alex.

Meg and Alex loved visiting Granny. They enjoyed swimming in the pond, discovering animal tracks in the woods, and baking cookies. They didn't mind that Granny never turned on the TV.

"It's so nice to sit together and talk," Granny always said.

"We always have such a nice time with Granny," thought Meg as she watched Granny wrap more yarn around the needles. "I wish we had something nice to give her."

Mimi stretched out a paw and swatted the yarn. "Don't ruin Granny's pretty sweater," scolded Meg as she pulled the cat away. She looked at Granny's work. "I wish I could knit like you, Granny," she said.

"Do you want to learn?" asked Granny. "I'd be delighted to show you."

Meg nodded her head. Granny took a ball of yarn and some needles from her basket and demonstrated how to start the first row.

Meg frowned over her needles as she twisted yarn around them. She didn't notice when the yarn rolled off her lap, but Alex did.

"This is perfect for making knots!"

Granny picked up the yarn. "That's for Meg's knitting," she said. "I'll get you some string to practice with later."

By the end of the evening, Meg had knit six wobbly rows.

"Keep practicing," Granny said. "Soon you'll be knitting like an expert!"

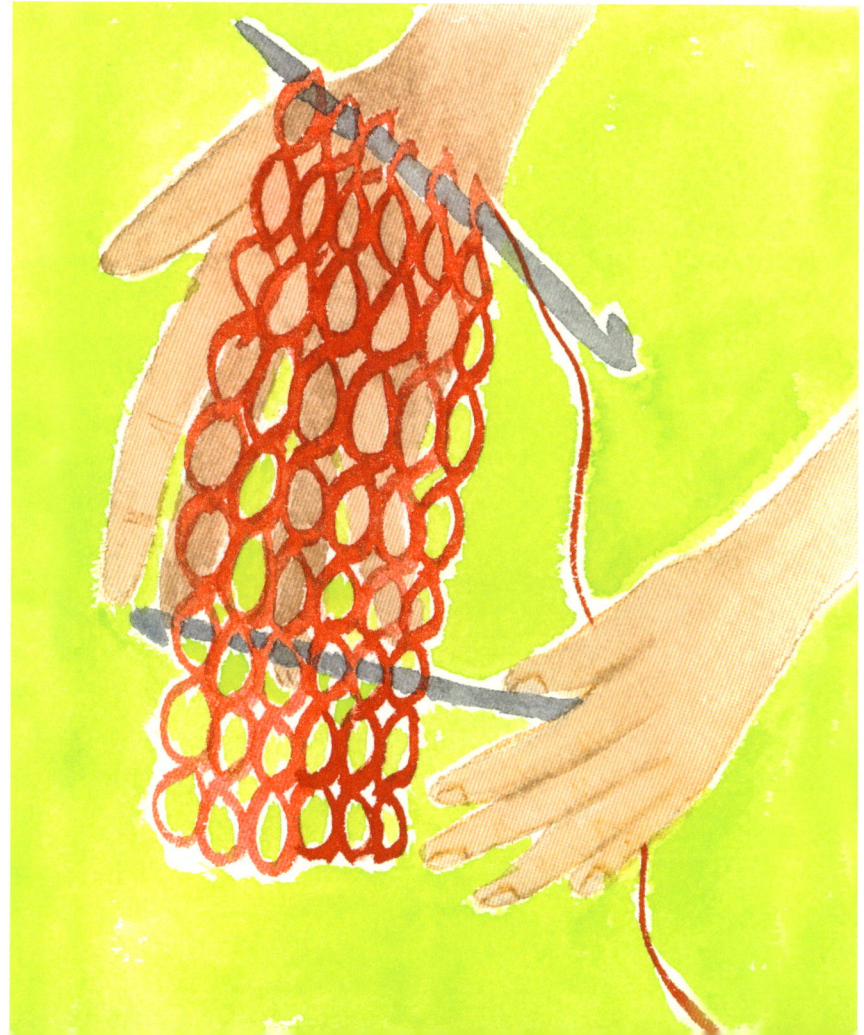

CHAPTER 2 MISSING!

The next morning, Meg found Granny in the garden.

"Shhh," said Granny. "Listen."

Meg heard a sweet whistling sound. Then she saw a bright flash of orange in the apple tree.

"Those are Baltimore orioles," said Granny. "They often make nests around here. I don't know where that one lives." They listened to the whistling sound together. "Oriole nests are interesting," Granny added. "They're like long socks."

"I wish I could see one," said Meg.

"We'll look later," said Granny. "Right now, it's time for breakfast."

After finishing her meal, Meg sat down to knit. By lunchtime, her rows were straight and even.

"I bet I could make a scarf now," she thought.

Then she had an idea. "That's it!" Meg exclaimed. She ran to find Granny.

"You know that basket of extra yarn you have with all the colors left over from your projects?" Meg asked Granny. "Can I use some?"

"I suppose so," said Granny. "What do you want it for?"

"It's a surprise."

Meg took the basket and her needles and went to sit under Granny's apple tree. She spread out the yarn on the bench. The rich colors were a stark contrast to the deep shade of the tree.

"How pretty!" exclaimed Meg. "And I think it's enough to make a scarf for Granny." She picked up a length of yellow yarn and began to knit.

By the time Granny called her for dinner, she had finished a wide yellow strip. She chose some orange yarn from the basket. "I'll start with this tomorrow," she decided. "If I knit every day, I think I can finish before it's time to go home." She hid the basket under the bench and went inside.

Meg went outside early the next morning. But when she looked in the basket, something was wrong. The tiny ball of orange yarn was missing.

CHAPTER 3 · WHO IS THE THIEF?

"Someone stole my yarn!" complained Meg, "and I bet I know who it was." She ran furiously into the house. "Alex! Alex!"

Her brother was planted at the dining room table in front of *The Big Book of Knots*.

"Where's my yarn?" asked Meg.

"Huh? I don't have your yarn."

"Yes, you do. You took it to make knots."

"No, I didn't. Look! Granny gave me this." Alex held up a large ball of white string.

Meg sighed and walked slowly out of the house, letting the door slam behind her. She was sure she had left the orange yarn in the basket. She rambled over to the apple tree and peered beneath the bench once more.

"Who could have taken that yarn?" she wondered. The question sat in her mind like a heavy stone.

"Oh, well," she finally decided, "I think I still have enough for a scarf." She picked up a piece of blue yarn and started knitting again.

The next morning, Alex and Granny went to the woods to look for the oriole nest. Meg chose to stay behind.

"Are you sure you won't come with us?" asked Granny.

"Thanks, but I'm working on something," said Meg.

As soon as Granny and Alex were gone, Meg ran to the apple tree. It would be time to go home soon, and she had to finish Granny's scarf before she left. She decided to use the red yarn next, but when she looked in the basket, the red yarn was gone!

CHAPTER 4 🪶 THE NEST SOCK

Meg jumped up and ran into the house.

"Mimi!" she shouted. "Where is my yarn?"

Mimi looked up from the sofa sleepily. Meg suddenly remembered that Mimi wasn't ever allowed to go outside because Granny wanted to keep her away from the birds. She couldn't have taken the yarn.

"I'm sorry for yelling at you, Mimi," said Meg. Puzzled, she went back outside, chose a length of green yarn, and began knitting once more.

More yarn went missing every day after that, and Meg grew more and more frustrated each time. She was rapidly running out of yarn. She was also running out of time. It was almost time to go home, and Meg had only a short knitted piece to show for her efforts.

"I have nothing to give Granny," she sighed.

On Meg's last afternoon with Granny, the two went for a walk in the woods.

"Granny," said Meg, "I wanted to make you a special present. I tried to knit you a scarf, but my yarn kept disappearing."

"That's very sweet of you, dear," Granny said. Then she stopped and pointed at the trees. "What could that be?"

Meg followed Granny's gaze. A bizarre bag was hanging from a branch. It was twiggy and brown with a zigzag of bright colors decorating it.

"That looks like an oriole nest!" said Granny. "But where did it find all those colors?"

Meg's jaw dropped. "It's my yarn!" she shouted. "Look, there's the orange yarn and the red and the green! The bird stole my yarn to make its nest!"

Granny laughed. "It looks like we found the oriole nest and solved your mystery!"

Meg sighed. "I really did want to make you that scarf."

"It's all right," said Granny. "Our new friend made me a sock instead."

They both laughed.

"I love visiting you, Granny," said Meg, "and looking for bird nests and learning to knit."

"And I love having you here," said Granny. She gave Meg a big hug. "That's the best present of all."

NONFICTION ✦ BIRD NESTS

Written by Katherine Rawson

Chapter 1 Nests and Eggs.........................18

Chapter 2 Scrape Nests and Platform Nests........21

Chapter 3 Burrow Nests and Cavity Nests......... 24

Chapter 4 Cup Nests and Host Nests............. 26

Chapter 5 Unusual Nests....................... 29

GLOSSARY................32

CHAPTER 1 | NESTS AND EGGS

All birds lay eggs, and most birds lay their eggs in a nest. But just as there are many different kinds of birds, there are also many different kinds of nests.

A nest may be as simple as a scrape in the ground, or it may be as fancy as a finely woven cup of grass. Whatever type of nest a bird makes, the purpose of the nest is always the same: A nest keeps the eggs and the young birds warm and safe. It protects them from **predators** and from the weather.

The number of eggs in a nest depends on the **species** of bird.

A nest may hold as few as one or two eggs, or it may hold as many as ten or more. The parent birds **incubate** the eggs by sitting on them to keep the eggs warm until they hatch. In some species, only the female incubates the eggs. In other species, the male and the female take turns. In a few species, just the male incubates the egg.

Eggs may hatch in two weeks or less, or they may take a month or longer. Some baby birds are ready to leave the nest soon after they hatch. Others stay in the nest until they **fledge**. They stay until they have feathers and can fly.

Nesting Information

SPECIES	Number of Eggs	Days to Hatch	Days to Fledge
American Crow	4–5	18	35
American Robin	4	13	15
Bald Eagle	2	35–40	65–70
Barred Owl	2–3	31	32
House Wren	5–8	12–15	15
Ruby-Throated Hummingbird	2	14–16	21

CHAPTER 2 SCRAPE NESTS AND PLATFORM NESTS

Scrape Nests

A scrape nest is the simplest kind of nest. It is just a dent scraped into the ground. Sometimes it is lined with grass, feathers, or small stones. Sea gulls, falcons, ostriches, and many ducks make scrape nests.

A scrape nest sits out in the open. It holds the eggs, but it does not hide them from predators.

In some scrape nests, the eggs are hidden by **camouflage**. They have colors and spots that help them blend in with their surroundings.

Platform Nests

Platform nests are mostly flat like a platform. A shallow dent in the center holds the eggs. The nest is made of sticks and may be lined with soft materials, such as grass and feathers.

Platform nests are often built in high places, such as ledges or large trees. That way, the eggs and babies are hard for predators to reach.

Eagles, herons, and ospreys make platform nests. Sometimes a pair of birds uses the same nest year after year. They add on to the nest each year, and it can soon become quite large. A typical bald eagle nest might be 5 or 6 feet wide and about 3 feet tall.

CHAPTER 3 BURROW NESTS AND CAVITY NESTS

Burrow Nests

Some birds, such as kingfishers, dig their own burrows. Kingfishers make their nests in the banks of rivers or streams. They like to be near the water where they fish. The kingfisher parents dig into the dirt with their beaks and feet to form a burrow 3 to 7 feet long. Then the mother kingfisher lays her eggs deep inside the burrow.

Other birds, such as burrowing owls, usually do not dig their own nests. Instead, they use old burrows made by other animals. The owls scrape out the burrow with their feet to make the nest more comfortable for themselves. A pair of owls might nest in the same burrow year after year.

Burrowing owls line their nests with **dung**. The dung attracts beetles, which make a tasty meal for the owls.

Cavity Nests

A cavity is a hole, and a tree cavity is a good place for a nest. Like a burrow, it protects the eggs from predators and from the weather. In the desert, some birds nest in the cavities of cacti.

Some cavity nesters make their own holes. Others use holes made by other animals. Cavity nesters include woodpeckers, chickadees, and parrots.

CHAPTER 4 | CUP NESTS AND HOST NESTS

Cup Nests

Many birds make cup nests. They use grass, twigs, moss, and other materials to form a nest into the shape of a cup.

The female robin makes her nest on a tree branch. First, she forms the nest with grass and twigs. Then she adds mud to strengthen it and lines the inside with dry grass.

Barn swallows build their nests in barns and sheds, under bridges, or in caves. The nests stick to the side of a wall and are made of mud mixed with grass. The inside of the nests is lined with grass and feathers.

The female oriole makes a special kind of cup nest that hangs from a branch like a sock. She weaves the nest with grass and strips of bark. She may also use bits of string, yarn, or hair. Then she lines the nest with grass and feathers. From start to finish, it takes her about two weeks to make the nest.

Host Nests

A cowbird is another bird that uses a cup nest, but it does not make the nest itself. Instead, it uses a host nest. This means that the cowbird lays her egg in another bird's nest.

The host bird incubates the egg and feeds the baby. Often the baby cowbird grows faster than the other birds in the nest, so it gets more attention from its host parents.

Penguin Nests

Most penguins make their nests by building up a small pile of pebbles. A small dent at the top holds the eggs. Emperor penguins, however, have no nest at all. Unlike other penguins, they do not lay eggs during the warm summer weather. Instead, the female emperor penguin lays a single egg in the middle of winter. Then the male penguin incubates the egg by holding it on his feet.

GLOSSARY

camouflage
coloring that helps an animal hide

dung
solid waste (poop) from an animal

fledge
to grow feathers for flying

incubate
to keep eggs warm until they hatch

lichen
a type of plant that grows on trees and rocks

predators
animals that hunt

species
a type of animal or plant

Hummingbird Nests

Hummingbirds build tiny cup nests less than 2 inches wide. The nests are so small that you might look at one and not even see it. Hummingbirds make their nests with bits of leaves, bark, and the silk from spiderwebs. They cover the nests with **lichen** as a form of camouflage. The finished nests look like a bit of lichen on a tree branch.

CHAPTER 5 UNUSUAL NESTS

Hornbill Nests

A hornbill is a bird with a funny-looking bill and an unusual type of nest. Hornbills keep their eggs and babies safe by sealing up the nest with the mother hornbill inside!

The nest is in a hollow tree. The male and female work together to build a wall of mud. The female stays inside the nest, and the male feeds her through a small opening in the wall.